*For Nancy Lohman Staub—*
*and to all those who love and care for the wild things*
*of this earth, including, of course, the children*

Requests for permission to make copies of any part of the work
should be mailed to the following address: Permissions Department,
Harcourt, Inc., 6277 Sea Harbor Drive, Orlando, Florida 32887-6777.

www.harcourt.com

Library of Congress Cataloging-in-Publication Data
Staub, Leslie, 1957–
  Bless this house/Leslie Staub.
    p.  cm.
  Summary: A nondenominational, ecological bedtime prayer
  celebrating home, family, and all the creatures of the world.
    1. Children—Prayer-books and devotions—English.  [1. Prayers.]  I. Title.
    BL625.5.S73  2000
    242'.82—dc21    98-51473
    ISBN 0-15-201984-7

First edition
H G F E D C B A

*Printed in Singapore*

*The illustrations in this book were done in oil on gessoed paper.*
*The display lettering was done by Judythe Sieck.*
*The text type was set in Stempel Garamond.*
*Printed and bound by Tien Wah Press, Singapore*
*This book was printed on totally chlorine-free Nymolla Matte Art paper.*
*Production supervision by Pascha Gerlinger*
*Designed by Judythe Sieck*

# Bless This House

THIS BOOK BELONGS TO:

# LESLIE STAUB

**HARCOURT, INC.**

*San Diego    New York    London*

Bless
this house

and bless
Bless the big
blue-white

this room.
bright
moon.

Bless my mom
and bless my dad,

even when they
make me mad.

Bless the bed where I sleep.
Bless my pillow
soft and deep.

Bless my window opened wide.
Bless the creatures who
live outside.

Bless chipmunks
and bluebirds, squirrels
and raccoons,

toucans, tigers,
bats and baboons.

Bless barkers
and tweeters,

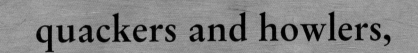

quackers and howlers,

trumpeters, yappers,

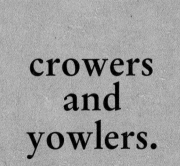

crowers
and
yowlers.

Bless them
in forests,

in ponds,

and on plains.

Bless even the ones
with really
small brains.

Bless the small plankton.
Bless the great whales.

Bless starfish
and minnows and
slimy sea snails.

Bless *all* of
the creatures who
swim in the
sea.

Bless dolphins
and penguins and fishes
and…

Bless us with kisses
and plenty of hugs.

Bless every last one of us—

even the bugs.

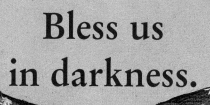

Bless us
in darkness.

Bless us with light.

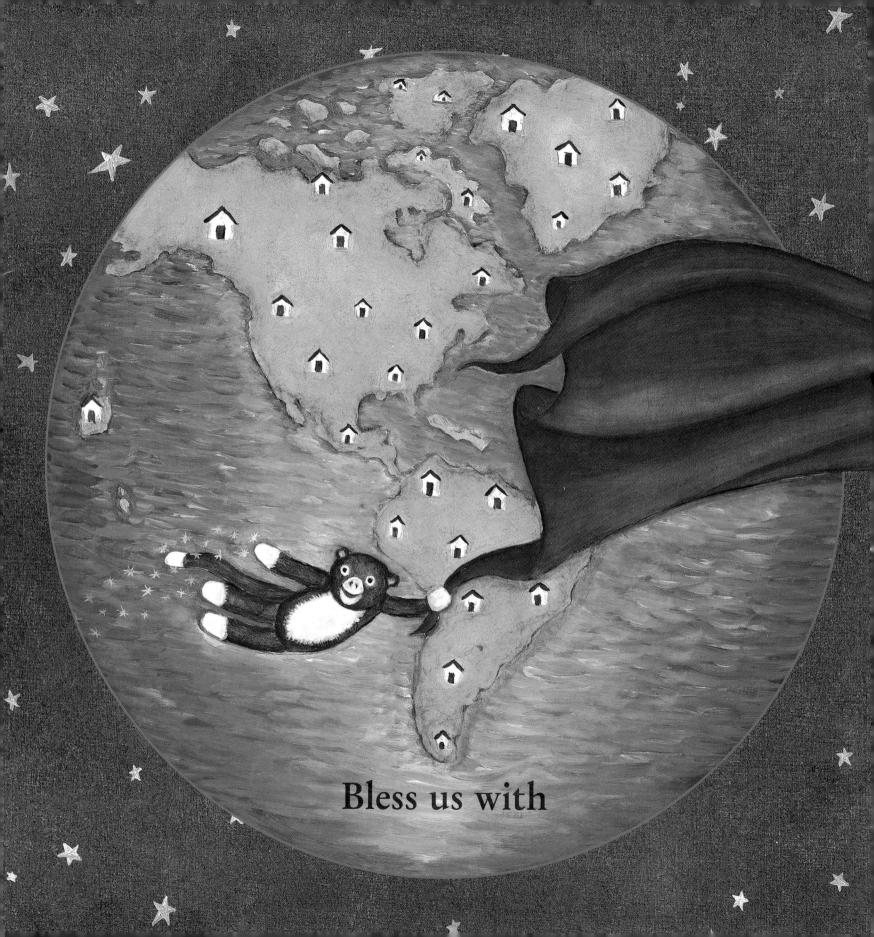

Bless us with

sweet dreams...

...all through the night.